Sovereign Frequency

The System of Emotional Mastery, Financial Clarity,
and Conscious Leadership

by A. J. Moore

ISBN (Paperback): 979-8-9933001-7-7

Sovereign Frequency
The System of Emotional Mastery, Financial Clarity,
and Conscious Leadership

Copyright

Dedication

For every person who carried too much weight alone.
May this book return you to your power.

Preface

Preface

There comes a moment in every life when the noise becomes too loud to ignore,
a moment when the pressure around you stops sounding like urgency and starts sounding like distortion,
a moment when you realize that survival is no longer enough, you need clarity, direction, and a way to reclaim yourself.

This book begins at that moment.

Not in crisis, but in recognition.
Not in collapse, but in awareness.
Not in fear, but in awakening.

You are not here because you lack strength.
You are here because you have carried too much weight alone.

Somewhere along your path, the world taught you to equate busyness with value, urgency with responsibility, instability with failure.
But none of that is truth.
Those are corrupted fields, emotional scripts written by systems that never had your peace in mind.

Sovereign Frequency is not a theory, it is not an ideal, it is not another demand for you to "do more" or "be stronger."

It is a system, a living architecture of clarity, designed to return you to the one thing you were never meant to lose:

Yourself.

This book will not shout at you, it will not rush you, it will not overwhelm you.

It will guide you, it will steady you, it will speak to you the way clarity speaks, calmly, consistently, and with purpose.

You will learn how to understand your field, debug your reactions, reset your mind, rewrite your emotional code, anchor your identity, and project a frequency the world cannot shake.

You are not here to become someone new.
You are here to remember who you already are.

Let us begin.

— A.J. Moore

Table of Contents

Introduction

The Architecture of Self

Most people live inside fields they never built,
they wake up in environments shaped by other people's
expectations, other people's demands, other people's
fears.
They react to pressure that isn't theirs.
They carry emotional weight they never agreed to.
They misinterpret signals because no one taught them
how to read the field.

As a result, they move through life with scrambled
emotional code, corrupted meaning, unstable financial
decisions, inconsistent boundaries, fractured identity.

And the worst part?
They think it's normal.

It isn't, it never was.

There is nothing normal about living in a constant state
of urgency.
There is nothing normal about tying your self-worth to
productivity.
There is nothing normal about feeling responsible for
everyone's reaction to your truth.

These are symptoms of a corrupted field, not a flawed person.

The Sovereign Frequency System exists to correct that.

Across this book, you will learn five essential architectures:

1. Field Corruption Index (FCI), how to detect emotional, financial, and psychological distortion.

2. Field Reset Protocol (FRP), how to interrupt looping patterns and restore clarity.

3. Field Compiler (FCX), how to rewrite meaning so that your identity commands your reality.

4. Field Anchoring Engine (FAE), how to lock sovereignty into your nervous system until it becomes automatic.

5. Reality Output Engine (ROE), how to create outcomes, stability, and opportunity through frequency-based leadership.

You will not be asked to push harder, you will be asked to move clearer.
You will not be asked to dominate, you will be asked to calibrate.
You will not be asked to fight, you will be asked to understand.

This book does not teach force.
It teaches field mastery.

Your field determines your frequency, your frequency
determines your reality, your reality determines your
life.

And once your frequency is sovereign,
nothing external can override you again.

Let's begin the architecture.

Chapter 1 — The Nature of Fields

Every person, every space, every decision, and every
moment operates inside a field.

A field is not mystical, it is not abstract, it is not
something only the spiritual or the scientific understand.

A field is simply the invisible environment of emotion,
expectation, and meaning that surrounds you.

It is the operating system of your life, always running,
always influencing your reactions and choices, even
when you don't realize it.

Most people feel fields, but cannot translate them.

They say things like:
"I don't know why this made me anxious,"
"Something feels off,"
"They drained my energy,"
"I can't think clearly."

They are describing the field, but without the language.

A field has three components:

1. Emotional Charge, the feeling present in the environment.

2. Assigned Meaning, the interpretation your mind assigns.

3. Identity Response, the version of yourself that steps forward.

If the emotional charge is corrupted, the meaning becomes distorted, and your identity responds from survival instead of sovereignty.

When you understand fields, you stop reacting and start interpreting,
you stop absorbing and start discerning,
you stop losing yourself and start leading yourself.

A sovereign life begins with one truth:

Your field is more important than your circumstances.

What you feel is data, what you interpret is code, what you embody becomes reality.

And the moment you learn how to read the field, you learn how to change your life.

Chapter 2 — How Fields Shape Identity

There is a quiet truth most people never learn:
Your identity isn't who you are, it's who your field
allows you to be.

Not permanently, not eternally, but moment to moment,
breath to breath.

Identity is not a fixed structure, it is a response pattern
you learned from the fields you survived.

If you grew up in chaos, you learned hypervigilance.
If you grew up unseen, you learned invisibility.
If you grew up responsible for others' emotions, you
learned self-erasure.
If you grew up with criticism, you learned to shrink.
If you grew up with pressure, you learned to brace.

None of these are personality traits.
They are field adaptations.

And when the field changes, or when you change your
field, your identity changes with it.

This is why the same person can be confident at work
but terrified at home,
calm in crisis but anxious in stillness,
strong in solitude but unsure in relationships.

Identity responds to environment.
Environment responds to meaning.
Meaning responds to the field.

When the field is corrupted, your identity becomes
distorted.
When the field is clean, your identity becomes
sovereign.

Most people don't realize how deeply the field dictates
identity.
They say things like:
"I always shut down in arguments,"
"I lose myself in relationships,"
"I panic around money,"
"I can't think under pressure."

But none of that is "just how they are," it is how their
field shaped them.

A corrupted field restricts your identity.
A sovereign field reveals it.

The Three Ways Fields Shape Identity:

1. Emotional Compression:
When a field is heavy, your identity begins operating in
survival mode.
You become reactive, defensive, avoidant, or exhausted.
Not because you're weak, but because compression
collapses clarity.

2. Cognitive Limitation:
Fields influence what your mind is able to perceive.
Corrupted fields narrow the mind.
Clean fields expand it.

3. Identity Compression or Expansion:
Fields decide which version of you comes forward.
Corrupted fields activate the anxious or reactive self.
Sovereign fields activate the calm, decisive, intuitive
self.

You are many things, but your field determines which
version becomes active.

The Identity Paradox:
You think you need self-improvement, but what you
need is field improvement.
You think you need more discipline, but what you need
is less distortion.
You think you need more confidence, but what you need
is clarity.

Identity is revealed through clean fields.

You can't fix identity from inside a corrupted field.
You fix the field, and identity aligns itself.

The First Identity Lesson:
Your identity is not who you are, it is who you've had to
be.
But Sovereign Frequency is who you choose to be.
And once you choose it, the field will follow.

Chapter 3 — The Source of Corruption

Every corrupted field begins the same way, with a mismatch.

A mismatch between what something is, and what you were taught it means.
This is the birthplace of distortion.

Human beings do not suffer because of events alone, they suffer because of the interpretations stitched onto those events.
Interpretations handed down by family, culture, survival, or systems that never asked if the meaning fit your truth.

Fields become corrupted when the meaning assigned does not match the reality experienced.

Corruption is not the event, it is the meaning fused to it.

The Four Sources of Field Corruption:

1. Emotional Overload:
When emotions are too strong to process, the mind compresses meaning to survive.
Compressed meaning is often distorted, creating shortcuts like:
"This always happens,"
"I can't handle this,"
"I have no options."
These shortcuts become corrupted code.

2. Environmental Misalignment:
If the environment does not match your truth, your
nervous system adapts to the environment, not to your
truth.
Chaos teaches the body hypervigilance.
Urgency teaches the body to distrust calm.
Pressure teaches the body to brace.
Your field becomes shaped by what you survived, not
what you needed.

3. Inherited Scripts:
Some corruption is generational, inherited fear, inherited
scarcity, inherited silence, guilt, or pressure.
You can feel corruption that never originated with you,
because fields transfer through proximity.

4. Systemic Conditioning:
Systems teach emotional lies:
"Your productivity is your worth,"
"Your debt defines your responsibility,"
"Your speed determines your value,"
"Your compliance measures your goodness."
Repeated long enough, these merge with identity.

The Hidden Mechanism, Emotional Debt:
You learned to feel guilty for resting, ashamed for
needing, responsible for others' reactions, pressured to
fix everything, afraid of disappointing systems that never
protected you.
This emotional debt becomes code.
And you pay for it with peace, clarity, boundaries, self-
worth, and nervous system regulation.

Corruption is not evidence of failure, it is evidence of survival.

You were adapting, not breaking.
Now you have the system to see, reset, and rewrite your field.

Chapter 4 — The Field Corruption Index (FCI)

Most people feel corruption long before they can name
it.
They know something is wrong, they just don't have the
language to explain why.

The Field Corruption Index (FCI) is the diagnostic tool
of the Sovereign Frequency System.
It detects distortion in real time, before it becomes panic,
spiraling, or self-doubt.

Corruption is predictable and measurable.
Once you learn the signs, you will never misunderstand
yourself again.

FCI is built on four universal markers, four "flags" that
reveal when the field has become compromised.

FLAG 1 — LOOPING:
Repetitive thoughts or emotions not connected to new
information.
If guilt, fear, shame, or dread repeat without resolution,
the mind is cycling corrupted code.
Looping is not a message, it is a malfunction.

FLAG 2 — LAG:
Hesitation, fog, or confusion that does not match the
moment.
This indicates a field mismatch, where the nervous
system tries to run old code in a new environment.

FLAG 3 — RESOURCE DRAIN:
Severe energy loss, emotional depletion, or sudden
exhaustion disproportionate to the moment.
A corrupted field siphons energy like corrupted software
drains battery.

FLAG 4 — IDENTITY OVERRIDE:
The most severe corruption, when the field attempts to
rewrite who you believe you are.
This includes feelings of unworthiness, pressure, guilt,
or a sense that you must prove or fix something.

SUMMARY:
Looping → distorted repetition.
Lag → hesitation without logic.
Drain → disproportionate energy loss.
Override → identity distortion.

One flag means the field is compromised.
Two means it is actively corrupting clarity.
Three requires immediate reset.
Four means you are no longer in your identity, but in
survival code.

The next step is clearing corruption through the Field
Reset Protocol (FRP).

Chapter 5 — The Field Reset Protocol (FRP)

A corrupted field cannot be argued with, reasoned with, or overpowered by force or discipline.
A corrupted field must be reset.

The Field Reset Protocol (FRP) is the emergency stabilizer of the Sovereign Frequency System.
It interrupts distorted meaning, restores breath, reclaims identity, and returns the field to neutral before action.

FRP is simple, fast, and powerful.
Use it in conversation, financial stress, conflict, panic, confusion, or identity pressure.

STEP 1 — INTERRUPT THE LOOP:
Corruption thrives on repetition.
Break the cycle by naming the distortion:
"This is not my voice,"
"This pressure is not my identity,"
"This reaction is not truth."

STEP 2 — RESET THE BREATH:
Breath shifts the body out of survival mode.
Use:
Inhale 4,
Hold 2,
Exhale 6,
Repeat twice.

This lowers adrenaline, restores clarity, and signals safety.

STEP 3 — REASSIGN MEANING:
Ask:
"What is actually happening?"
Remove fear, assumption, and inherited scripts.
Return the moment to truth:
Bills are numbers,
Emails are information,
Silence is processing, not rejection,
Delay is timing, not failure.

STEP 4 — RECLAIM AUTHORITY:
Anchor sovereignty:
"I choose my response,"
"I act from clarity, not chaos."

Boundaries strengthen, urgency loses grip, emotional debt collapses.

STEP 5 — CHOOSE THE SMALLEST POSSIBLE STEP:
Choose the smallest step that gives the largest clarity:
Open the envelope,
Read the message once,
Write the number down,
Take a breath,
Say "I'll revisit this at 3 p.m."

Small steps interrupt overwhelm and rebuild direction.

FRP SUMMARY:
1. Interrupt the Loop,
2. Reset the Breath,
3. Reassign Meaning,
4. Reclaim Authority,
5. Choose the Smallest Step.

Use FRP anytime panic rises, clarity drops, pressure hits,
or identity wavers.
FRP returns you to yourself before the situation tries to
define you.

Next: The Field Compiler (FCX).

Chapter 6 — The Field Compiler (FCX)

Most people do not suffer because of events, they suffer because of the meaning they assigned to those events. Meaning is the hidden architect of identity, determining interpretation, reaction, and behavior.

The Field Compiler (FCX) transforms intention into identity, identity into behavior, and behavior into reality. Where the Field Reset Protocol clears distortion, the Field Compiler replaces the old code with truth.

THE COMPILER FORMULA: INPUT → MEANING → OUTPUT

INPUT: What you intend.
MEANING: How you interpret.
OUTPUT: What you do.

Identity creates meaning, meaning creates behavior, behavior creates reality.

STEP 1 — SET THE INPUT (Intention):
Ask:
"What outcome do I want my energy to create?"
Not to fix or impress, but to create clarity, resolution, boundaries, peace, or truth.
Intention is architecture.

STEP 2 — RECODE THE MEANING
(Transformation):

Override old interpretations.

Examples:

"This is a threat" → "This is information."
"I'm behind" → "I'm calibrating."
"I messed up" → "I'm adjusting."
"This is urgent" → "This requires clarity."
"This defines me" → "This reveals me."

Meaning determines behavior.

STEP 3 — CHOOSE THE OUTPUT (Behavior):
Choose the action that matches your intention:
A calm tone,
A delayed response,
A boundary,
A pause,
"I'll respond at 3 p.m."

This creates outcomes that reflect identity, not fear.

THE COMPILER IN ACTION:
A bill arrives.
Old meaning: "I'm failing."
New meaning: "This is a number."
Output: Write the number down, act calmly.
New reality: clarity, direction, options.

SUMMARY:
To change the field, rewrite the code.

To change your reality, rewrite the meaning.

Your frequency becomes self-authored.
Your reality becomes self-directed.

Next: The Field Anchoring Engine (FAE).

Chapter 7 — The Field Anchoring Engine (FAE)

Once you reset the field and rewrite the meaning, the next step is to make the new identity permanent.
Most people calm their thoughts, but their nervous system continues running old code.
Change dissolves because nothing is anchored.

The Field Anchoring Engine (FAE) binds new meaning, new behavior, and new identity into your body, mind, and environment until it becomes your default state.

THE FOUR ANCHORS OF THE FAE:

ANCHOR 1 — SOMATIC LOCK (The Body Anchor):
Use the body to stabilize the field.
Somatic locks include the 4–2–6 breath, dropping your shoulders, relaxing your jaw, unclenching your hands, touching your sternum, or straightening your spine.
Each one signals:
"You are safe. Respond from sovereignty."

ANCHOR 2 — COGNITIVE KEY (The Mental Anchor):
A phrase or belief that instantly reorients the mind.
Examples include:
"I choose my frequency,"
"Pressure is not a command,"
"Nothing defines me without my permission,"
"Still mind, strong field."

These keys interrupt emotional hijacks.

ANCHOR 3 — BEHAVIORAL MICRO-MOVE (The Action Anchor):
A small action that signals sovereignty:
Pausing before replying,
Opening the email,
Writing a number down,
Asking a clarifying question,
Saying "not today,"
Or choosing a time to respond.

Micro-moves turn clarity into progress.

ANCHOR 4 — ENVIRONMENTAL SIGNAL (The External Anchor):
Your environment communicates with your nervous system.
Anchor identity through:
A candle for decision-making,
A journal for clarity,
A grounding chair,
A focus playlist,
A consistent scent,
A clean or intentional workspace.

HOW THE ANCHORING ENGINE WORKS:
Repetition creates identity,
Consistency creates sovereignty,
Embodiment creates permanence.

Each anchor strengthens regulation, clarity, and identity.
When all four activate:
Somatic lock,
Cognitive key,
Micro-move,
Environmental cue,
You enter Sovereign Lock, the state of unshakeable,
self-generated frequency.

SUMMARY:
Somatic Lock — calm the body,
Cognitive Key — align the mind,
Micro-Move — direct behavior,
Environmental Signal — stabilize the field.

Together, these create automatic sovereignty.

Next: The Reality Output Engine (ROE).

Chapter 8 — The Reality Output Engine (ROE)

Most people think reality is something they experience, but sovereign individuals understand that reality is something they produce.
Not by force or domination, but by frequency.

Once you understand your field, reset distortion, recode meaning, and anchor identity, your nervous system emits a different signal into the world.
That signal changes how people respond to you, what opportunities appear, and how reality organizes itself around your presence.

THE OUTPUT EQUATION: Identity → Frequency → Behavior → Reality
Identity produces frequency, frequency produces behavior, behavior produces outcomes, outcomes create reality.

THE THREE OUTPUT CHANNELS:

1. Cognitive Output — Clarity → Direction:
Clear minds create clear decisions.
Clarity leads to efficient problem-solving, stronger intuition, and simplified plans.

2. Emotional Output — Identity → Atmosphere:
Your emotional state broadcasts to the environment.
Calm regulates others, consistency attracts respect, sovereignty creates ease.

3. Behavioral Output — Action → Reality Shaping:
Micro-actions grounded in sovereignty reshape external reality:
Small choices,
Aligned timing,
Conscious boundaries,
Intentional communication.

THE FOUR OUTPUT MODES:

MODE 1 — STILLNESS EXECUTION:
Calm, precise, slow, deliberate action.
Strategic thinking without panic.

MODE 2 — CALM ASSERTION:
Clear truth, steady tone, firm presence.
Leadership without aggression.

MODE 3 — SOVEREIGN NEGOTIATION:
Urgency loses power.
Pressure cannot influence you.
Clarity becomes leverage.

MODE 4 — RESONANT CREATION:
Ideas flow,
Opportunities find you,
Abundance aligns,
Synchronicities increase.
Reality mirrors your coherence.

OUTPUT ACTIVATOR:
"I decide what my field produces."
This command shifts the nervous system from reaction to authorship.

SUMMARY:
Cognitive Output → direction,
Emotional Output → atmosphere,
Behavioral Output → reality,
Four Modes → influence,
Activator → sovereignty.

The Reality Output Engine is how your internal
Sovereign becomes visible.

Next: Applications of Sovereign Frequency.

Chapter 9 — Applications of Sovereign Frequency

Sovereignty is not a theory, it is a practice. This chapter applies the full system to the areas where people lose themselves most: finances, relationships, work, and emotional pressure.

SECTION I — FINANCIAL SOVEREIGNTY:
Calm is the foundation of all financial clarity. Numbers are neutral, timing is strategy, and emotional debt is not financial debt.
Use FRP: interrupt the loop, breathe, ask "What is actually happening?", anchor identity, take the smallest step.

SECTION II — RELATIONAL SOVEREIGNTY:
Boundaries are instructions, not walls. You are responsible for clarity, not for others' reactions.
Pause before responding. Do not negotiate from stress. Never shrink to preserve connection.

SECTION III — WORKPLACE SOVEREIGNTY:
Urgency is not authority. Stillness Execution stabilizes meetings. Saying "I'll review this and respond" reclaims time and clarity.
Burnout is a field failure, not a personal failure.

SECTION IV — SOVEREIGNTY UNDER
PRESSURE:
Pressure reveals coding. FCI detects corruption, FRP
resets, FCX rewrites meaning, FAE locks identity, ROE
produces calm action.
You shape pressure, pressure no longer shapes you.

APPLICATIONS SUMMARY:
Financial Sovereignty → clarity,
Relational Sovereignty → identity,
Workplace Sovereignty → authority,
Pressure Sovereignty → mastery.

Sovereign Frequency simplifies everything. Simplicity
creates space for power.

Chapter 10 — The Sovereign Declarations

A person becomes sovereign the moment they choose to stop letting the world define their identity.
Not through conflict, not through rebellion, but through clarity.
Sovereignty is not dominance, it is self-authorship.

Declarations are commands to your field, boundaries to your environment, codes for your nervous system, and signatures for your identity.
They rewrite your internal narrative and reorient your external reality.

DECLARATION 1 — "I choose my frequency."
Not my fear, not my past, not someone else's urgency.
Choice before reaction, identity before emotion.

DECLARATION 2 — "Pressure is not a command."
Pressure is noise, presence is signal.
Move at the speed of clarity.

DECLARATION 3 — "Nothing defines me without my permission."
Identity is self-authored.

DECLARATION 4 — "My emotions are data, not destiny."
Emotions inform, they do not command.

DECLARATION 5 — "I am allowed to pause."
Stillness is intelligence.

DECLARATION 6 — "I do not negotiate from chaos."
Regulate before you respond.

DECLARATION 7 — "I can handle truth without losing myself."
Truth is direction, not threat.

DECLARATION 8 — "My presence stabilizes the room."
Your nervous system becomes leadership.

DECLARATION 9 — "I do not abandon myself."
Self-honoring is the first sovereignty.

DECLARATION 10 — "I decide what my field produces."
Identity commands reality.

HOW TO USE THE DECLARATIONS:
Use them at the start of the day, before conversations, during pressure, or when identity wavers.
Speak them calmly, breathe slowly, embody them gradually.
They rewire the nervous system and anchor sovereign identity.

Next: The Sovereign Practices.

Chapter 11 — The Sovereign Practices

Sovereignty is not sustained by intention alone, it requires practice.
Practices transform identity from an idea into a reflex, embedding Sovereign Frequency into daily life.

PRACTICE 1 — THE MORNING FIELD CHECK:
Before checking the world, check your field.
Ask:
1. What is the emotional tone of my body?
2. What meaning is my mind defaulting to?
3. What version of me is awake right now?

PRACTICE 2 — THE BREATH RESET (4–2–6 Pattern):
Inhale 4, hold 2, exhale 6.
Use before conversations, bills, messages, or pressure.
Breath resets the nervous system and restores clarity.

PRACTICE 3 — THE SOVEREIGN PAUSE:
Pause before reacting or explaining.
This triggers FCI, FRP, FCX, and FAE.
Stillness becomes strength.

PRACTICE 4 — THE "SMALLEST STEP" RULE:
Do one small step:
Open the email,
Write the number,
Ask the question.
Small steps create clarity and momentum.

PRACTICE 5 — THE BOUNDARY BREATH:
Before saying yes or no, ask:
"Is this aligned with my identity?"
Calm = yes, tight = no, foggy = not yet.

PRACTICE 6 — THE SOVEREIGN JOURNAL
ENTRY:
One sentence daily:
"Today, my field produced ________."
This builds authorship and conscious creation.

PRACTICE 7 — THE ENVIRONMENTAL RESET:
Clean one thing daily.
Environment instructs the nervous system.

PRACTICE 8 — THE EVENING SOVEREIGN
CHECK:
Ask:
1. Where was I sovereign today?
2. Where did corruption try to override me?
3. Which declaration do I need tomorrow?

SUMMARY:
Morning Check — identity first,
Breath Reset — nervous system first,
Pause — clarity first,
Smallest Step — momentum first,
Boundary Breath — truth first,
Journal — authorship first,
Environment — alignment first,
Evening Check — integration first.

These practices create self-generated sovereignty.
You become the architect of your own field.

Next: The Sovereign Scripts.

Chapter 12 — The Sovereign Scripts

Every field is shaped by language. The way you speak to yourself, to others, and under pressure influences your frequency. Most people speak from distortion, but sovereign individuals speak from clarity, intention, and authority.

SECTION I — SOVEREIGN SELF-TALK:
"I'm allowed to slow down."
"I don't need to solve everything right now."
"My feelings are valid, but they are not instructions."
"Let me get clarity first."
"I honor my pace."

SECTION II — SOVEREIGN BOUNDARY SCRIPTS:
"That doesn't work for me."
"Here's what I can do."
"I'll need time to think about that."
"Let's revisit this when emotions settle."
"No, thank you."

SECTION III — SOVEREIGN NEGOTIATION SCRIPTS:
"What problem are we actually trying to solve?"
"What options haven't we considered?"
"I hear your urgency, but I will move at the pace of clarity."
"Let's move this from emotion to information."
"Here is what I require."

SECTION IV — SOVEREIGN DE-ESCALATION SCRIPTS:

"Let's take a breath before we continue."
"I don't want to respond from emotion, so I'm going to pause."
"I understand what you're feeling, let's slow down."
"Let's separate facts from feelings."
"We're not in conflict — we're in communication."

SECTION V — SOVEREIGN FINANCIAL SCRIPTS:

"Let me review the numbers first."
"I will handle this at _______ time."
"I need clarity before I commit."
"What's the most important part for you?"
"I'm not rushing. I'm recalibrating."

SECTION VI — SOVEREIGN RELATIONSHIP SCRIPTS:

"I want to understand you. Can you tell me what you're feeling?"
"I'm listening. Go slowly."
"I need space to process that."
"I care about this, so I want clarity."
"I'm not abandoning myself to keep the peace."

SECTION VII — SOVEREIGN PRESSURE SCRIPTS:

"I choose clarity over urgency."
"Let me breathe first."
"I'm not required to react."
"I will respond when I'm regulated."
"I decide what this moment becomes."

SUMMARY:
Sovereign Scripts regulate your field, anchor identity, guide communication, stabilize environments, and influence outcomes. You do not speak to win, you speak to align and remain sovereign.

Next: The Sovereign Affirmations.

Chapter 13 — The Sovereign Affirmations

Affirmations are emotional instructions that teach your nervous system how to interpret reality.
They regulate your field, anchor truth, and strengthen identity under pressure.

SECTION I — AFFIRMATIONS FOR EMOTIONAL CLARITY:
"I can feel this without losing myself."
"My emotions are messages, not commands."
"Clarity returns when I breathe."
"Stillness is where my wisdom lives."
"I allow myself to slow down."

SECTION II — AFFIRMATIONS FOR IDENTITY:
"I am not behind. I am aligning."
"I honor who I am becoming."
"I deserve to take up space."
"My presence is valuable."
"I trust myself to choose wisely."

SECTION III — AFFIRMATIONS FOR BOUNDARIES:
"My boundaries protect my identity."
"I do not apologize for my needs."
"I have the right to pause before responding."
"I choose relationships that honor my presence."
"No is a complete frequency."

SECTION IV — AFFIRMATIONS FOR PRESSURE:
"Pressure is not my guide."
"Urgency does not control me."
"I act when my field is stable."
"I remain whole under intensity."
"This moment will not define me."

SECTION V — AFFIRMATIONS FOR FINANCIAL
PEACE:
"Numbers do not measure my value."
"I make financial choices from clarity, not fear."
"My money follows my intention."
"I release guilt connected to money."
"I am learning, adjusting, and becoming wise."

SECTION VI — AFFIRMATIONS FOR
RELATIONAL SOVEREIGNTY:
"My voice matters."
"I can love without abandoning myself."
"I am safe to speak clearly."
"I give and receive from alignment."
"I choose relationships that nourish my field."

SECTION VII — THE ANCHOR AFFIRMATION:
"My field belongs to me."

Affirmations stabilize emotion, identity, boundaries,
pressure, finances, and relationships.
They prepare the field for action and reinforce sovereign
identity.

Next: The Sovereign Covenant.

Chapter 14 — The Sovereign Covenant

A covenant is not a promise made under pressure or a resolution born from fear.
It is a conscious alignment, a declaration of identity, a commitment to your future self, and a stabilization of your field.
It is the moment Sovereign Frequency becomes not simply a practice, but a person you are.

THE SOVEREIGN COVENANT:

I. FIELD
I honor my field.
I recognize that my field shapes my thoughts, emotions, decisions, and reality.
I take responsibility for keeping my field clean, calm, and sovereign.

II. IDENTITY
I author my identity.
I will not allow fear, pressure, urgency, or expectation to override who I choose to be.

III. TRUTH
I honor truth, not distorted truth born from pressure, but clarity born from stillness.
Truth is my compass, stillness is my foundation.

IV. BREATH

I return to breath before I return to fear.
My breath is my anchor, my reset, and my doorway back
into myself.

V. BOUNDARIES

I do not abandon myself.
My boundaries protect my identity, guide my
relationships, and safeguard my peace.
I choose connections that honor my presence.

VI. MEANING

I choose the meaning I assign to my experiences.
I refuse inherited scripts, distorted interpretations, or
corrupted emotional code.
I interpret life from clarity, not fear.

VII. PRESSURE

Pressure does not command me.
Urgency does not define me.
Expectation does not move me.
I act from alignment, not adrenaline.
I choose clarity over chaos.

VIII. RESPONSIBILITY

I am responsible for my field, not for the reactions or
projections of others.
I offer clarity, not compliance.
I offer honesty, not self-erasure.

IX. CREATION

I am the architect of my energy.
I shape my reality with intention, not impulse.
My frequency is my contribution to the world.

X. SOVEREIGNTY
My field belongs to me.
My identity belongs to me.
My peace belongs to me.
My future belongs to me.
I stand in the full truth of who I am, without apology,
without shrinking, without fear.
This is my covenant.
This is my alignment.
This is my sovereignty.

THE COVENANT PRACTICE:
Repeat the covenant silently in the morning, aloud when
needed, in writing once a month, or in breath when
pressure rises.
A covenant is not a contract with perfection, but a
commitment to awareness.
Awareness, sustained and sovereign, creates a life only
you can author.

Next: The Integration Map.

Chapter 15 — The Integration Map

The Sovereign Frequency system becomes most powerful when all components work together. Integration is not doing everything at once, but activating the right part of the system at the right moment.

THE INTEGRATION FLOW — The 7-Step Sequence:

1. NOTICE — What is happening in your body, thoughts, and field?

2. IDENTIFY — Which FCI flags are active?

3. RESET — Interrupt → Breath → Meaning → Authority → Small Step.

4. REWRITE — Intention → Meaning → Output.

5. ANCHOR — Somatic Lock → Cognitive Key → Micro-Move → Environmental Signal.

6. PROJECT — Clarity Output → Emotional Output → Behavioral Output → Output Mode.

7. REFLECT — "What did my field produce?"

THE REAL-WORLD INTEGRATION GRID:

I. INTERNAL INTEGRATION:

Emotion → Looping → Breath → "My feelings are data" → Somatic Lock → Stillness Execution.

Self-doubt → Lag → "What is actually happening?" → "I am aligning" → Cognitive Key → Calm Assertion.

Fear → Override → Breath → "Fear is information" → Micro-Move → Resonant Creation.

II. RELATIONAL INTEGRATION:

Conflict → Drain → Pause → "We're in communication, not conflict" → Boundary Breath → Calm Assertion.

Pressure → Override → "Pressure is not a command" → "I decide my pace" → Cognitive Key → Sovereign Negotiation.

Heavy caring → Looping → Breath → "I can love without abandoning myself" → Environmental Signal → Stillness Execution.

III. FINANCIAL INTEGRATION:

Anxiety → Lag → "Numbers are information" → "This is a number, not a judgment" → Micro-Move → Clarity Output.

Urgency → Override → Breath → "I move at the speed of clarity" → Somatic Lock → Sovereign Negotiation.

Guilt → Looping → "Guilt is not guidance" → "I am aligning, not failing" → Cognitive Key → Resonant Creation.

IV. ENVIRONMENTAL INTEGRATION:

Overwhelm → Drain → Smallest Step → "I change the field one piece at a time" → Environmental Reset → Stillness Execution.

Heavy space → Lag → Breath → "This space responds to me" → Candle / Music / Scent → Emotional Output.

Grounding need → Override → Pause → "My environment reflects my peace" → Grounding Chair → Calm Assertion.

THE DAILY INTEGRATION CYCLE:

Morning — Field Check, Declaration, Breath Reset.

Midday — Smallest Step, Micro-Move, Sovereign
Script.

Evening — Sovereign Check, Journal Sentence, Breath
Reset.

Integration creates self-generated sovereignty.
You do not react to life, you coordinate it.

Next: The Master Diagram.

Chapter 16 — The Master Diagram

A system becomes powerful when it becomes simple.
The Master Diagram condenses every component of
Sovereign Frequency into one unified map.
It shows how corruption begins, where clarity returns,
how identity stabilizes, and how sovereignty activates.

```
                         SOVEREIGN FREQUENCY
SYSTEM


    ------------------------------

                              [ FIELD ]
                                 |
                                 v

    +-------------------------------+
                    |       FIELD CORRUPTION INDEX
    |
                    |    Looping • Lag • Drain •
Override

    +-------------------------------+
                                 |
                                 v

    +-------------------------------+
                    |       FIELD RESET PROTOCOL
    |
                    | Interrupt • Breath • Meaning
• Action • Step

    +-------------------------------+
                                 |
                                 v

    +-------------------------------+
```

```
                    |          FIELD COMPILER |
                    | Intention → Meaning → Output |
+---------------------------------+
                                  |
                                  v

+----------------------------------+
                    | FIELD ANCHORING ENGINE |
                    | Somatic • Cognitive • Action • Space |
+----------------------------------+
                                  |
                                  v

+----------------------------------+
                    |    REALITY OUTPUT ENGINE |
                    | Clarity • Atmosphere • Action |
                    | Modes: Stillness, Assertion, |
                    | Negotiation, Resonant Creation |
+----------------------------------+
                                  |
                                  v

+----------------------------------+
                    |    SOVEREIGN DOCTRINE |
                    | Declarations • Scripts • Cov. |
+----------------------------------+
                                  |
                                  v
```

```
+------------------------------------------+
                |            SOVEREIGN PRACTICES
|
                | Morning • Breath • Pause • Step
• Bound.  |
                | Journal • Reset • Reflection
|

+------------------------------------------+
                                   |
                                   v

+------------------------------------------------
------+
           |                 INTEGRATION MAP
|
        | Internal • Relational • Financial •
Environmental   |

+------------------------------------------------
------+
                                   |
                                   v
                FINAL STATE: SOVEREIGN
IDENTITY

----------------------------------
                Calm • Clear • Anchored •
Self-Authored
```

Chapter 17 — Closing Note & Future Vision

You have reached the final chapter of this work, but this is not the end of your journey.
It is the beginning of the life you were meant to live.

Sovereign Frequency is not a philosophy or coping mechanism, it is a way of being.
A way of thinking, breathing, responding, and creating.
It is a return to clarity, identity, emotional intelligence, and power.
You did not come this far to become a better version of your old self.
You came here to meet the self you were always becoming.
You are becoming the field others stand in.
People will calm around you.
Rooms will shift around you.
Opportunities will open around you.
Your presence will stabilize your environment.
Your nervous system becomes leadership.
Your clarity becomes influence.
Your presence becomes anchor.
Your future is sovereign.

From now on, you do not abandon yourself to survive moments.

You do not shrink to protect others.
You do not rush to earn approval.
You do not break to appear strong.
You move from embodiment, clarity, identity, and sovereignty.

When the world tests you:
You breathe.
You pause.
You slow down.
You choose clarity.
You reset.
You rewrite.
You stand.
You offer calm.

A vision for what comes next:
Imagine a world where people regulate before reacting,
families communicate in truth,
communities stabilize each other,
leaders guide through presence,
and decisions are made from clarity, not fear.

This is not fantasy, this is the world built by individuals who master their field.
You are the beginning of that world.

Your final charge:
Honor your field.
Respect your breath.
Protect your identity.
Expand your frequency.

Your field belongs to you.
Your life belongs to you.
Your future belongs to you.

You are sovereign.
Now go live sovereign.

— A.J. Moore